All Done Day

How to Win at
Everyday Parenting

Everybody loves
an All Done Day!

Ann Lahm

Ann Lahm

ISBN: 978-1-7349337-1-0

Dedication

I dedicate this book to all parents who have decided to take this job of parenting seriously. You have hardened yourself against the protests of your children and popular cultural trends. You know that you may be your child's friend someday, but for now and for always, you are their parent, loving and firm. You are the ones who are leaning in closer for instructions and inspiration from all the right sources. For making this brave commitment and sacrifice, I am your biggest fan!

> "Your greatest contribution to the universe may not be something you do, but someone you raise."
>
> —*Andy Stanley, speaker, author, and pastor*

Table of Contents

Foreword

I am a business owner and dad to four children. Owning and running my own business has had its ups and downs, but I can honestly say the biggest challenges I've ever faced have come at the end of the day. When our four kids were younger, I'd often come home to a tired and frustrated wife and a chaotic house. It was a busy and challenging time for the Lahm family. Our kids needed "something more" to put them on a better path to success. We tried many things until it finally became clear that we needed a paradigm shift in our home—a new way of thinking and doing.

At work, I lived in a world of measurements and processes, identifying problems and working to solve them. These were at the core of the skills that I used every day. As it turned out, our family was a far more complex organization. The people involved were my own flesh and blood, and my heart was wrapped around each one. At home, if they did not perform, I could not fire them! Ann was a capable and loving mom, but she could not solve this alone.

As a team, Ann and I came up with an experiment that changed our home and the trajectory of our kids' lives. The All Done Day plan brought a dynamic to our home that was both surprising and amazing. It became a way of life, stood the test of time, and grew with each of our children. Read on! *All Done Day: How to Win at Everyday Parenting* is the story of how it worked for us and how you can tailor it to meet the needs of your family.

All the best to you and your family,
Steve Lahm

Introduction

I have experienced the heart-draining frustration and hopelessness of trying to parent without a plan that works. Summer vacation was the worst. It always came with the advertisement of great weather, a break in the school routine to enjoy outdoor activities, and a more carefree pace to life. I expected my kids to wander aimlessly through summer, sleeping in and leaving a trail of messes all day long—and that's exactly what they did! I finally decided I didn't want to be a first-rate summer activities director. I wanted my kids to grow and thrive and grow some more. And not just during the summer, by the way, but all year long. Was this too much to ask, I wondered?

Our family was in need of a change; a new approach to life. So, with the help of my husband, Steve, we came up with a daily plan for each of our children, along with a list of rewards they could earn as they completed their plans. This was when the All Done Day plan was born! It created purpose for each child's day, inserting some order while also allowing us great teaching opportunities in the areas of discipline and character development. The kids felt like winners as they achieved goals they were working toward. They often helped set the goals and always made the choice for their rewards.

For the first time, my children were in control of whether they were succeeding. It gave them a feeling of empowerment and immense pride. My desperate reach for summer survival turned into a normal part of our family's way of operating for many years, and not just in the summer months. Parenting became more pleasurable for Steve and me because it wasn't just up to us to make sure things got done; they were actively invested too. Steve and I could be more focused on encouraging the kids' progress and celebrating their successes than on moment-by-moment motivation.

The peace and order our All Done Day plan brought to our home was incredible, but it was not nearly as rewarding as the victories we have observed now that they are each in their twenties. Our grown children have developed good habits and share positive stories of these experiences with others. Why? Because it was a powerful experience for all of us. That is why I am so pleased to be able to share it with you!

As you work to employ the All Done Day plan in your home, you will be blessed with opportunities to learn more about each of your children, their personality challenges, where they are today, and where they could be tomorrow. Because moms love to talk about their children, and I am no different, here is a glimpse of who my children were at the launch of the journey, and where they are today!

Meet First Born, Lauren

Our oldest was most happy when curled up on a comfy couch, engrossed in a book like Harry Potter, to the exclusion of playing outside or getting much else done. She preferred to wear pajamas all day, while reading. All Done Day pushed Lauren to have structure, which gave her direction on physical activity, piano practice, completing household tasks, and thinking outside of herself. Service opportunities and jobs provided positive learning experiences for Lauren.

Where is she today? Lauren completed dual degrees in chemistry and biochemistry and works in her field. She gives of herself as a mentor to teen girls at her church. Physical activity, in the form of CrossFit has become a regular part of her week. (You go, girl!)

Meet Middle Child, Barret

This child was the most naturally helpful of our children. Barret was the one I could count on to jump in and help me in a pinch, and with no complaining. This does not mean he was disciplined or self-directed, though. He was energized by time spent with his friends. All Done Day helped Barret buy into the completion of his tasks so that he could reap the benefits, such as sleepovers with his friends. Since music practice was part of his plan, he became a better violinist and musician.

Where is he today? Barret earned a degree in Finance and is working as a financial analyst. He still enjoys time with friends, and especially his wife. He is a guy who is perpetually managing a task list at work and at home.

Meet Middle Child, Mitchell

This is the child who would be so focused that it was hard to draw him out of his own little world. Mitchell loved video games and Legos and would do either one for hours. Mitchell would not do any tasks without specific direction. All Done Day helped Mitchell develop the framework he needed to balance a day of practicing trumpet, completing homework, keeping in shape for soccer, and helping to keep our house in order.

Where is he today? Mitchell has demonstrated laser focus during his PhD program in computational chemistry. He balances classes, Teaching Assistant responsibilities, and long research hours—after making his bed each morning!

Meet Last Born, Megan

The youngest of the tribe watched how everyone else was doing things. As a child, Megan made her own path. She loved friend time and was skilled at avoiding "girl drama." She always enjoyed music, both playing and listening. All Done Day caused Megan to see the value of getting things done. It also helped her to envision the reward. She really benefitted from having order in her day. The structure helped her in her high school years to carry a heavy load of classes, work, sports, and music, while maintaining friendships.

Where is she today? Megan is completing a degree in computer science. She has juggled school, orchestra, intramural soccer, and the responsibilities of a teaching assistant and a facilities shift manager. She mentors freshman women and frequents the dean's list.

After bringing the All Done Day plan into your family's life, I can virtually promise that:

- you will NOT be doing everything for your children.

- your children will have a clear plan for their day.

- you will instill an opportunity for daily success.

- you will experience natural teaching activities.

- you will get to know each child better.

- you will encourage goal setting and goal achieving.

- you will instill a great work ethic.

- you will prove to your children the benefit of good choices.

- you will allow your children to suffer from natural consequences.

- you will stop being a "nag" and let the plan do the talking.

- you will learn to focus on the positives.

- you will be motivated to complete your own daily tasks.

- EVERYONE WILL WIN!!

All Done Day will give you the tools and the encouragement to implement this for your family. It worked in my home, and it will work in your home too!

Let's get started!

Chapter 1

ALL Done Day –
More Than Just Chores

Most chore systems are doomed to fail before they begin because the bigger picture has not been defined. If a child is assigned a task list, he or she may complete it if the reward is sweet enough or to avoid consequences, but the child's and parent's efforts will soon fizzle. They always do. Children lose momentum because they are immature, lack the ability to see long-term benefits, and are not given ownership. If children are doing something to please a parent, they are not mature enough to keep that up. They are unable to see the big picture.

My husband and I wanted more than a chore system. We needed an intentional plan of action. In response, we developed the All Done Day plan. We were able to insert purpose, give our kids goals to work toward, encourage character development, spur them toward a desire for excellence, and help them grow to become better people and confident leaders! The completion of their daily plans was just the beginning of all the wonderful benefits we all experienced.

For everyone, adults included, life is more than just completing a list each day. It is looking ahead and setting goals based upon what is most important to you. It is about achieving goals, but all in the context of everyday life. This is what *All Done Day* helps to implement.

We have all seen "that kid" who throws a tantrum when they don't get to do it their way or don't get what they want at the store. Most upsetting of all is when "that kid" is your kid! No parent sets a goal to raise a spoiled child, and yet, we do. Before we know it, we find ourselves giving into our child's demands, being inconsistent, giving out empty threats, saving them from consequences, bribing them, giving them too much control, allowing disrespect, and giving them too many material possessions.

How many times did I find myself picking up the dropped coats and shoes from the floor or yelling, "This time I really mean it!"? How many times did I bribe them or jump in to save or relieve them from consequences that they really deserved? How many times did I buy them things that they did not need or deserve? Too, too many times, I am afraid.

Even the most well-intentioned parents
find it hard to stay strong over the years
and across the span of all their children.
It is like running an ultramarathon!

And how about the ways that I have helped my child solve their problems, like being the air traffic controller for their present and future relationship problems? How many times was I far more stressed out about the science fair project than they were? (And yes, I stayed up and glued things to the poster board to help make the A possible.) How many times did I ask a question of a teacher, coach, or restaurant server that they could and should have asked on their own?

In *The Opposite of Spoiled*, Ron Lieber writes "Spoiled children tend to have four primary things in common, though they don't all have to be present at once: They have few chores or responsibilities, there aren't many rules that govern their behavior or schedules, parents and others lavish them with time and assistance, and they have a lot of material possessions."[1]

---

[1] *The Opposite of Spoiled*, Ron Lieberman.

Using this yardstick, even the best of parents would have to admit they have been guilty of spoiling their children. It is not something they set out to allow in their parenting. It creeps in situation by situation. Parents have good intentions and love their children dearly, but they have unknowingly fostered behavior that paves the way toward entitlement. Consider my decision to help with the science fair poster board. I justified that not only because I wanted my child to get a good grade, but also because I felt he needed to get enough sleep.

The good news is that using the blueprints of the All Done Day plan, parents can reverse the direction of unintentionally spoiling their children and begin building discipline, purpose, and responsibility into their kids. By defining what it is that you want to foster in your children, the character qualities you want them to exhibit, and the skills you believe are important in successful adults, you will have a clearer path for how to impart them to your children.

Steve and I also wanted to keep our children's hearts at the center of our parenting. In the creation of our All Done Day plan, we enjoyed the benefit of learning more about each child's heart as we searched for their motivators and points of discouragement. We studied them to determine what goals we thought would be beneficial for them to work towards. Completing the daily plan was NOT more important than each child's heart. But, in saying this, we also recognized that our children were not yet mature and needed us to be loving overseers of their days and their lives.

Steve and I were looking for ways to give our children something more than status quo parenting. We looked at many of the parents around us, and they seemed to be as lost as we were! But we were determined to move forward and learn. We soaked up a lot of parenting advice and resources and were able to sift out what we thought were some winning schools of thought.

One idea that stuck with us was from a FamilyLife Parenting Conference. Founders, Dennis and Barbara Rainey, suggested creating a "target" for your children, keeping certain goals in mind that you want them to achieve as they moved from childhood to adulthood. For example, one of the targets we set for our children was to develop a good work ethic. This was a goal that could not be accomplished by reading books. And they certainly could not accomplish this by watching us do their jobs for them! Children learn by doing; they learn by working! If parents do everything for their kids, they will not get a sense of hard work, and we've all seen this proven out through real-life examples. All Done Day created the chance for our kids to work hard and to gain over time various rewards and praise from others who noticed. It is a very gratifying feeling to hear a child's teacher, coach, or employer tell you that your child has a good work ethic, the very target we had established for them years prior.

Another target we identified was that our children would develop a love for music. So, part of that path was to have each of the kids learn to play an instrument. Some of them played several instruments. They took private lessons. They practiced. They were expected to grow in musical knowledge and ability. That takes discipline, and it takes time. It takes a daily commitment. They did not always love the work that was needed, but there were rewards along the way. Being in a band, orchestra, or choir provided enjoyable learning and performance experiences. It gave them an instant place to "belong" and to be contributors to something bigger than themselves. They were given opportunities to go places on tours or for competitions that they would not have gone otherwise. They gained personal confidence. It gave them opportunities to work through all that goes into performing in front of an audience. They learned that there is gratification in making beautiful music and that it brings pleasure to many who come to hear them perform. They also learned the value of "giving back." As hard as it was at times to be the parent enforcing the practice sessions, it helped toughen our resolve as parents, and we do not regret the appreciation our kids gained for music and the fine arts. I have a hunch our children will decide to have this as a target for their children as well!

Could we have called our children to excellence without creating the All Done Day plan? Some parents will reason that doing chores should be the focal point and required of every member of the family and an end in themselves.

I agree with children needing to learn personal responsibility, but they still have to be taught and mentored over the course of many years toward ultimate life goals. Successful parents learn how to motivate their children and to use those motivators to direct them toward enriching daily plans. This is what will prepare them for everyday achievements; setting them up for ongoing success in life.

I maintained an active private piano studio for over twenty years. It is always exciting to start a new student, and to see his or her excitement for the new adventure. Several months into the lessons, when the novelty has worn off and the real work has set in, most students would quit if left to themselves. The support of parents and wise educators is monumental in the lives of kids. We must be there to motivate and walk alongside our children, encouraging them to work toward meaningful discipline. In music specifically, they learn much more than just the mechanics of playing a piece. They learn discipline. They learn sacrifice. They learn delayed gratification. They learn how to set a goal and reach it. They learn how to handle frustration and setbacks. Whether music, sports, or a myriad of other activities, children learn life skills that will follow them and set them up for future successes.

The All Done Day plan helped us to keep the end goal in mind on a daily basis. When our children were inching closer toward college, we found a video curriculum called

CollegeReady which helped address the many joys and challenges of college life. The most valuable exercise in the course was to picture where they wanted to end up at the end of their college years in key areas, like academics, friendships, dating, social fun, and spiritual life. This came back to the idea of having a target to shoot for, an idea our family was familiar with already. Having daily tasks that were linked to life targets was key in our four children realizing their life goals.

Chapter 2

An All Done Day WILL Make a Difference!

We've all worked alongside people who grew up with a daily routine of work. They are the ones who always have their "sleeves rolled up," and you can't help but feel inspired to join them in their can-do attitude.

U.S. Navy Admiral William H. McRaven spoke to the May 2014 graduating class of the University of Texas at Austin and said, "If you want to change the world, start by making your bed!" What a great charge to young people–to all people! He suggested making it the first task of your day. Many parents have given up on this expectation for their children.

What if you could help your children incorporate certain tasks in their day that would become second nature and "stick" for life?

When you get up and immediately make your bed, you:

- have one task already completed

- have a better chance of NOT getting back into bed

- begin moving forward

- have a living space that instantly looks better

- create a better feeling about the possibilities of your day

- never have to feel embarrassed by "drop-in" company, especially your mom

- take a step toward keeping the rest of your room neat

- reduce stress when there is some order in your living space

- make bedtime more inviting by getting into a "made" bed

- put good bookends on the beginning and ending of your day

The biggest win is the immediate feeling of accomplishment from a completed task which can lead to many other completed tasks in your day. My friend, Susanna, said that when she went through chemotherapy for breast cancer, getting up and making the bed made a statement that she was living as healthy a lifestyle as possible. If the bed was made and she was dressed, Susanna was not tempted to rest in bed, even if she went to another room to rest on a couch. It propelled her forward and helped her to not wallow in her condition. Susanna gets up these days, makes her bed, gets dressed, and is enjoying remission from cancer!

Judy Dutton, in *Psychology Today*, notes that "in a survey of 68,000 people by Hunch.com, 59 percent of people don't make their beds. 27 percent do, while 12 percent pay a housekeeper to make it for them. She noted, "Here's what disturbed me: 71 percent of bed makers consider themselves happy, while 62 percent of non-bed-makers admit to being unhappy. Bed-makers are also more likely to like their jobs, own a home, exercise regularly, and feel well rested, whereas non-bed-makers hate their jobs, rent apartments, avoid the gym, and wake up tired. All in all, bed makers are happier and more successful than their rumple-sheeted peers. Since these factors show correlation but not causation, this does not mean that non-bed-makers can't be happy and successful, but the odds are stacked against them. And it makes sense, since an organized environment can positively impact our mental state—and given it only takes 30 seconds, it could lend a small sense of accomplishment at the very start of the day. So maybe I'll try it. My Mom would be proud."[2]

Most people value productivity, and if it can begin first thing in the morning, an All Done Day is definitely within reach!

Little things you can teach your children, such as making their bed and staying active, will become great life habits. When our family would go on a long car trip (and we took many of these), Steve would, without fail, let our kids know that before anything else happened after arriving home, everyone would work together to get the car unpacked. It was SO helpful, especially the next day, to know that there was not a mess left in the car that no one was motivated to take care of. Using the parent and kid power available to get it done in record time was a sure WIN! I can't wait until my children are parents themselves and carry on these "work-together traditions." It should be part of their DNA by now!

---

[2] Dutton, Judy,"Make Your Bed, Change Your Life," http://www.psychologytoday.com (August 16, 2012)

Okay, time out. Don't think that this all happened with smiles and a happy soundtrack. Many times, it was accompanied by groans and whining that would tempt most parents to say, "Oh, just forget it!" Steve and I had to steel ourselves for the inevitable opposition. Of course, we were tired too. These are the teachable moments that foster stamina in parents and discipline in children. No matter who you are, you can't always do what you want to do. From a very young age, children can learn that along with something fun, like playing a game or taking a vacation, the clean-up at the end is always part of the activity. Instilling this expectation will help your children learn how to follow through. Looking ahead, this can teach them to clean up at a work site, be a better employee, or be a considerate roommate.

Chapter 3

An All Done Day Principle:
Work Is Important

Learning how to work is very important for every child, and we learned firsthand that it was important to build that into our All Done Day plan. So many parents are missing this! Many parents are spending time with their kids, encouraging them to be involved in activities such as sports or the arts, pushing them academically, and telling them to volunteer, yet the routine exercise of daily work is often overlooked. Those who can afford it seem willing to pay for ready-made meals or house cleanings in order to value the time spent on children's activities. We spare our children and ourselves work for a variety of reasons. From me, you will have no judgement, but let's ponder the importance of work.

In hindsight, I wish my mom would have had me do more work around the house. In her defense, my dad traveled a lot and with five kids, she often felt outnumbered. It was easier for her to "do it herself" than to put up with our complaining. Sorry for the grief, Mom! Dad was far more proactive in this area and he treated us all equally when it came to the outdoor chores. We all had our sections of the lawn to mow, and it was all hands on deck when there was snow to be shoveled, the driveway needed to be blacktopped, or the dock needed painting. And my dad's expectations were clear; he did not negotiate, at all.

I may have successfully dodged the indoor chore duty, but I missed a lot of learning because of it. When children are part of doing routine tasks, like cleaning the bathroom, emptying the dishwasher, mowing the lawn, vacuuming, and doing their laundry, they learn what goes into the day-to-day maintenance of a home. Children who grow up in a family organization that "gets things done" will transfer those skills to their dorm, their workplace, and even their own families someday. My daughter was amazed that the other college freshman in her dorm had not done a load of laundry until they were at college, staring at a pile of dirty clothes! She had been doing her own wash for years! Wait until your kids have roommates that were not taught how to clean up after themselves or how to do basic housekeeping tasks. You will hear lots of stories!

It is paramount that our children learn not to take for granted all that is done for them. They benefit from the completion of those tasks, so involving them in household upkeep and teaching them to be grateful for the help they receive are equally important.

If you do have a house cleaner, don't feel guilty as many families find this to be a lifesaver. I have had housekeeping help in certain seasons of my life, when I could afford it, and when it helped calm some chaos. Just make sure to save some tasks for the "home crew," and have your children take an active part in thanking the house cleaner for being a part of the team.

Julie Lythcott-Haims, author of *How to Raise an Adult*, and TED Talk presenter, proposes that doing chores at a young age increases the chance of future professional success. She says, "Chores help children to see the work that needs to be done and the initiative to do it." She goes on to say, "If kids aren't doing the dishes, it means someone else is doing that for them. And so they are absolved of not only the work, but of learning that work has to be done and that each of us must contribute for the betterment of the whole."[3]

One of the things we can and should be teaching our children to do is *work*. It can start with chores, but as they get older, real work in the order of a for-pay job should be added to the mix. Some of the work can be service projects, but an outside job will bring all kinds of new

---

[3] Julie Lythcott-Haims, *How to Raise an Adult*

experiences and challenges to work through. There are some that say kids today face too many pressures to succeed and they don't have time for a job as past generations did. I would argue that it is more important than ever for our kids to get and keep a job during their pre-college years. It might take some creativity to find the right fit or the right schedule, but job experience is crucial. If your teenager is really pinched for time, have him or her consider something small such as weekly babysitting, yard work, or tutoring. It will help teach time management, communication, and being accountable to others.

I love the story my pastor, Bob Merritt, told his congregation recently. I share it here with permission.

"I grew up rather poor, the son of a preacher—four siblings—a brother and three sisters. I had two pairs of pants to my name and switched them out when one got dirty. They were hand-me downs from my brother. There was no such thing as an allowance in our house. We worked as kids growing up. When I was eight years old, my Dad took me down to the Joliet Herald News in Joliet, Illinois, and he said, 'Bob wants a paper route.' And I said, 'I do?' So, I got hired as a helper for a kid named Ron. A year later Ron went to college and I took over his paper route and delivered papers every single day-seven days a week—for the next four years. At age thirteen, my Dad bought me a push mower. I mowed lawns for the next three or four years. I had ten lawns by mid-summer and my own lawn mowing business by age 13! When I was sixteen, one of the parishioners in my Dad's church had a painting business and my Dad said, 'Bob wants to paint houses!' I said, 'I do?' I didn't know the first thing about it! They took me over to a house, gave me a three-hour lesson on how to scrape, caulk, and paint–and that was it! Then they left me with an entire house to paint, at the age of sixteen. But by summer's end, I had painted three houses and banked $5,000 on my own. When I was eighteen, my parents drove me from Pittsburgh to St. Paul, Minnesota, for college. As soon as we unloaded my stuff in the dorm, Dad drove me over to Columbia Transit Bus Company and said, 'Bob wants to drive a school bus!'"

I asked Pastor Bob if he harbored any resentment about how his dad provided these "work opportunities" for him. He said he really valued having to go out and create possibilities for work. He said, "Don't wait for something to come to you; go out and get a job. It gave me a real can-do approach to work and life that I still carry with me today."

Steve and I purposely steered our kids into job opportunities. Lauren babysat and cooked for others. Barret worked for Dad's business, first scanning documents and later as a software tester. Mitchell worked stocking shelves in an office supply store, and Megan got a job during high school scooping ice cream.

**Living out your own life of work
is not enough to model for your children.**

They need to be invested in work of their own. This is where the life lessons will come, and it's where discipline and character will be built. The All Done Day plan can be the beginning of your training program of work for your children. It provides a framework and a purpose to create the daily discipline and character development that can lead to great, lifelong accomplishments.

Chapter 4

The "Secret Sauce": Associating Value to Tasks

SPOILER ALERT: What follows is the *All Done Day Secret Sauce.*

In many households today, there is a great struggle to get kids to take on tasks. It is easy and very common to think cold hard cash will motivate them. Yes, of course we tried that too, but here is what we learned. It became clear very quickly that each of our kids was motivated by different things. We had four "test cases" right under our roof, after all! We had one child who was VERY motivated by money. He would roll up his sleeves and dig into a chore when he was saving for something. When he felt his needs were all being met and there wasn't an immediate "wish list" item on his radar, he was not motivated to help. If I posted jobs with dollar amounts on them, the same one or two children would tackle them every time.

I recently heard a dad talking about how he had given his son $20 for some snacks at a basketball game he was going to watch with friends. His son spent the entire $20 that night! The following week, the same child was going skiing and he asked for money for snacks. Dad remembered that the son gets an allowance, so he told his son to use his own money if he wanted to buy snacks at the chalet. His son went into the kitchen, grabbed two packets of hot chocolate mix, and said, "I guess I'll just ask for some hot water!" Perspective changes when there is more ownership!

We had an allowance system to help our children learn how to manage money, but it did not depend upon merit. In addition, we developed the All Done Day plan and engineered incentives to help create more discipline in several aspects of our children's everyday lives.

The beauty of the plan is that even at a very young age, children can take ownership and begin to develop discipline in their lives.

I need to tell you very emphatically that tying completion to incentives was THE secret sauce to making All Done Day work. When our kids learned that they could earn things that they valued, they followed through! That's when Steve and I knew we were onto something that would work. Our kids became highly motivated and committed to the plan. We watched as they stopped at their bedroom doors to read their plan. Sometimes they got right to their list of tasks, and sometimes they decided to do them later, but more often than not, the tasks were completed by the end of the day.

Our kids were not left to guess our expectations because we had spelled them out. When they collected their All Done Day Coupons, there was a sense of accomplishment and pride. When they enjoyed one of the rewards that they worked for, like going out for a Daddy Donut Date, there was a heightened sense of enjoyment. The Daddy Donut Date was a favorite incentive when the kids were young…Let's just say Dad had to make himself available most Saturday mornings! The kids were not old enough to see the big picture of "why" we were doing all this. That would come later. For now, they were doing the work and gaining rewards for completing their plans. It was a win-win situation!

As our kids got older, the rewards grew with them. Instead of a Daddy Donut Date, we offered options like a trip to the pottery painting store. We were continually taking their pulse and appropriately adjusting their incentives list. You will need to know what is "trending" with your child. Even if a routine is good for me, I personally need to insert splashes of change or "something new" to keep me engaged. I guarantee you this will happen, and you will need to anticipate this and be ready to add twists, new ideas, or tweak the incentives to fit the direction of your child's current "sweet spot."

An important lesson I learned was to not give my children too much of the wrong things. One of my favorite ways to show love to people is to give gifts. Birthdays are never missed, and I love to give cards and little expressions that let them know I was thinking specifically about them. Like any parent, I wanted to be able to give my children the best the world had to offer, whether it was great experiences or cool stuff. I came to the realization, though, that if I met all of my children's desires, the All Done Day plan would not work.

Let me say that again. If you meet all your child's desires, the All Done Day plan will not work. As adults, when we have our eyes on something we want, we have to work for it. Often if it is an expensive item, we have to save and sacrifice to make the purchase a reality. The saving and sacrifice and work all seem worth it when we finally have that "prize" in our possession.

By not giving your children as much, you will create a hunger and a drive that will motivate them to work to earn those wish list items. And guess what? This is why the All Done Day works. Your child will learn to work and value the reward. Those items should become part of your child's All Done Day Incentive List. We found that the enjoyment we observed in our children was greater when they worked for the incentive than if we just provided it for them. Of course, you will not (and should not) incentivize all the fun in your home, but wisely observe what your children love to do or want to have and hold some of that back as incentives. It felt like we had a secret weapon when we saw our kids step up on a consistent basis, completing their All Done Day plans, saving up their coupons, and "buying" their favorite incentives.

We also became wiser about when and what we gave our children. My husband traveled a lot for his work, many times overseas. It would be fun to bring back something for each child when he went on a trip, but with four kids, the things that came back were often junky plastic toys. We decided to let them know that Dad was not going to always bring back gifts, but if he saw something that really fit a particular child, he would bring it home. With this new mindset, the gifts that did come home were far more memorable, not to mention Steve felt much less pressure while traveling. Many times, he would bring a gift the whole family could enjoy. The kids learned to welcome Dad home with "We missed you" instead of "What did you bring me?" The kids also learned not to expect to be treated the same. Aren't these such valuable life lessons? These just don't happen without intentional parenting.

Chapter 5

Another All Done Day Basic: Encouraging Our Children to Aim Higher

One of the important jobs that a parent has is to help their child grow and mature—to expand their knowledge, confidence, and abilities. Unfortunately, we often do not realize that in our methods or zeal, we are actually stunting their growth potential. There is a term we use for parents who are over-focused on their children: Helicopter Parents. Just like a helicopter, they "hover" over their children, making most of their decisions, micro-managing their time, and shielding them from consequences and disappointments. Or we become Lawn Mower Parents who mow down any obstacles in their children's lives. We mean well. I have been guilty of this at times, as most good-willed parents will be, but Steve and I made it our real aim to be parents who were focused on equipping our children. We wanted them to learn from a variety of experiences. We wanted to encourage our kids to aim higher, to learn how to work, and how to become "finishers." We were able to do that through their All Done Day plans.

Kids lack maturity, and left to themselves, they will not make wise or beneficial decisions much of the time. They do not understand the importance of learning and developing good character and strong work ethic. It is a parent's job to direct them toward meaningful activities, but not to completely control them. Whether you had parents who were great role models or not, the ball is now in YOUR court. If you are reading this book, I believe you are looking to intentionally build discipline and purpose in your child's life through a combination of teaching and nurturing. You might need courage to move forward on your ideas, or you might have plenty of desire but lack ideas. Either way, I commend you because any step forward is a good move! Taking advantage of opportunities to teach your children to work and learn will reap many rewards, some of which you will not see for many years.

Our own children were typical teenagers who drifted toward laziness when it came to everyday tasks and setting goals. We really did not want them to "miss out" on experiences that we knew would be enriching for them. Our local Rural Electric Association offered a Washington D.C. Youth Tour each summer, which provided an opportunity to see our government in action, shake hands with senators and members of Congress, and tour our nation's capital, while making friends from other parts of the country. An energy-related essay was required in order to be considered for this experience.

Have you ever tried to push an enormously heavy object up a hill? That is what it was like to get my kids to write essays! Adding to the pain of it all, we refused to help them write their essays. However, we did provide encouragement, proofreading, and prodding as the deadline approached. Three of our children applied for the trip experience, and two of them were selected for the Youth Tour in two different years. The one who was not selected for the trip later won a college scholarship through the same organization. Another essay.

I asked our adult children to look back on the experience and give some of their thoughts:

Son 1: "I think part of my lack of motivation in that instance was that I didn't truly think I would have a chance to win. I did not fully comprehend the true value of a trip like that due to my lack of maturity. I needed the push my mom gave me to finish the paper and would not have done so on my own. I would have lost out on an amazing experience. Basically, kids are kids and don't know how to properly prioritize and weigh costs and benefits. They need help deciding what to focus on and what to put their time into."

Son 2: "My brain had not made the connection that my hard work would lead to a big reward at the end, because

I had not yet experienced that at such a level. Also, if I remember correctly, I didn't really have confidence that I could win it! Those two things aside, I am incredibly thankful that my parents pushed me through."

As I read my sons' responses, it was apparent that not only did they lack the ability to grasp the concept of what they could attain by putting in some effort, but they also needed encouragement to "try" things. We dropped some balls along the way, no one can do it all! Remember, parents are learning, too. We will not do everything our children need, but what we do to encourage and teach them will not be wasted. Let's start by being realistic about what our children can (or should) strive for. Some of our children will never have what it takes to be a professional athlete, but there are big benefits to playing on a team. They may not become a world class musician, but they can develop a knowledge and love for music that will give them an enjoyable hobby or make them a more satisfied audience member in the future. They can learn to improve their abilities, contribute to a team, and grow mentally tough from training and competing. It's very difficult for enthusiastic parents to keep a lid on expectations that might be unrealistic, demotivating, or emotionally hurtful.

Daughter 1 did not apply for the Youth Tour trip, but I had a conversation with her since then, asking her if she resented the things we urged her to do and experience.

Her response was that she wished we had pressed her more!

> ## Our children need us to be calling them higher. This is one of our most important responsibilities.

If we had waited for our kids to go out and serve others, build academic skills in the summer months, or make the decision on their own to clean their room, we would have been waiting a very long time. By using the All Done Day plan to create a sense of routine and responsibility, our kids were not allowed to drift. Had we not encouraged our kids to write the essays, they would not have the experiences, memories, educational opportunities, and scholarships that they were able to enjoy. Do I feel badly they missed playing some video games to write those essays? Absolutely not!

With time, the All Done Day plan will help your whole family step up to a new level of performance, order, and awareness. As a parent, I found myself becoming much more productive because I was also working to accomplish my own plan. Before I devised my kids' plans, I tended to just respond to what was right in front of me, and that did not make me more efficient or organized.

Because it was a "thing" our family did, accomplishment became part of our way of operating. And it is so healthy when each family member has ownership of what they need to accomplish to meet their goals. This is what will groom them for bigger accomplishments in the future.

There is nothing so enjoyable as when the atmosphere of your home begins to change. A young mom named Elizabeth recently shared with me: "The best part of having your kids mop the floor is that when one of them starts to walk inside with muddy boots, the other ones yell that the floor was just cleaned. I don't have to say a word! It's amazing how when you have to clean something yourself, you work harder to keep it clean."

Chapter 6

What Do We Really Value?
Defining Targets

To create a purposeful plan for your child, it is very important that you are drawing from a master plan of what you want to create for your family and for your household. When we have a list of traits or skills that we feel are important for our children to embody or learn, we will have a better blueprint for how to help them develop those traits or learn those skills. Zig Ziglar aptly warned us, "If you aim at nothing you will hit it every time."

We may know in our heart what is important to us but have never verbalized it, shared it with our spouse, or taken time to plan how those values might affect our parenting going forward. Setting aside time to write out your family values or "targets" will give you a lens by which to make decisions. In two-parent families, it will be a learning exercise to see what is truly most important to each of you. Commit to listening to each other and the differing opinions that come from the culmination of your own life experiences, upbringing, and desires. Creating this list will allow you to lock arms and walk together and parent with purpose. If you are a single parent, you are strong and used to handling it all alone. However, I encourage you to seek the help and encouragement of a wise friend or mentor who can help you work through determining your family values and how to prioritize them in the midst of single parenting.

Approach this exercise with the understanding that your family values list will be fine-tuned as you start to walk this out. When you start down the path of determining what is important to you, it will lead to deeper reflection and greater intentionality. You will arrive at a clear vision of what is most important, but it will not happen overnight. You will start noticing things in your life that affirm what you have already listed, and you will likely take something off your list that you realize is unrealistic or not truly important. Feel the freedom to make changes but start somewhere. Don't be afraid to let your children see you work through this. It's not a sign of weakness, it's true leadership.

Verbalizing your values helps you to embrace those values and live them out in a meaningful way.

This is not the time to be frustrated with the time behind you, maybe years, that you feel you were not leading in the right direction. As I said, that is behind you and you have the power to change the direction of your parenting and your family. The All Done Day plan is transformational. It certainly was a leap ahead for our family.

After you go through the exercise of defining your family values, you can begin creating the personalized All Done Day plan for your child/children. It is interesting to see how assigning tasks takes on new significance when they are lined up with your list of family values. For example, one of the great motivators for putting together the All Done Day plan for our family was that we wanted each of our children to develop our family value of a good work ethic. To us, a good work ethic included learning skills like reliability, persistence, punctuality, adaptability, thoroughness, finishing what they started, and integrity.

When we laid out the individual plans, our expectations were communicated for how those traits would be measured. We didn't drop this on our children all at one time. We wove those valued traits into our everyday conversations to teach them what a "job well done" included. What does it mean to be punctual? It means getting somewhere before the starting time and being ready to go. It includes having what you need with you, such as athletic equipment, schoolbooks, pencils, music, enough money, and a good attitude.

As the kids got older, they also learned that their punctuality and preparedness affected those around them. These conversations we had with our children were rarely planned but took place during natural teaching opportunities. Steve and I were primed to be on the lookout for good points of entry to talk about these things. It was amazing how often the topic popped up. We found the best opportunities for these types of conversations were when an infraction of a trait affected our child. If a friend is late in arriving for an event and it frustrates your child, we'd take the chance to ask them, "How did it make you feel when your friend was late for something that was important to you?" It is an opportunity to point out that our actions do affect others. And you can also talk about what it means to be a good friend, showing grace to those who were late, for example, instead of just grumbling. When you are alert to these open doors, the situation can do the talking. They drive home the point more effectively than any lecture, big or small, ever could!

Chapter 7

What Motivates My Child?

It is pretty easy to think about tasks you want your child to accomplish each day, but it is more difficult to identify each child's motivators. This is an area in which many parents throw up their hands because they can't put their finger on what motivates their children. Many parents end up offering the same incentives to all. The rationale is that no one can say it's "not fair" if it's "the same." In the name of fairness, we end up creating an environment that can be both frustrating and demotivating.

Rarely do all children in a family respond to incentives in the same ways. One child is compliant because of being a natural rule follower, one child is motivated by praise, and another child tunes it all out because breaking the rules is, well, worth the thrill. Different children look at life in different ways. Hang on to your resolve and don't give up!

Every child is worth studying, and the most difficult are often the most tenacious, successful adults.

Work at it until you uncover their "currency!" It's important for parents to accept that what motivates you may not motivate your child. When you find the desired incentive, and every child has one, he or she WILL work for it!

Focus on one child at a time, and answer these questions:

What is one of their passions?

What makes them happy?

What kinds of things energize them?

What gets them up in the morning?

What will they drop everything for?

What demotivates them?

What do they ask to do more than anything else?

What do they naturally do well without much or any parent "pushing?"

What do they not do well, that requires extra effort from you and him?

You may need to take a few days and just observe how your child operates, using that question list to help you. It will be very enlightening to start to understand just who your child is, and what makes them "tick." Let me demonstrate how this exercise played out when we were determining what motivated each of our two sons. In these examples, you will see a snapshot of when each of them was 10 years old.

What are Barret's passions?	Spending time with friends and time with Dad with no siblings
What makes Barret happy?	Time with friends, riding bike, sweets, information and control (knowing what was for supper, or the agenda for the weekend)
What energizes Barret?	Time with friends, physical activity, and helping others
What gets Barret up in the morning?	He is a morning person, gets up with anticipation for the new day
What will he drop everything for?	A chance to do anything with friends, going on an errand with Dad, and candy/treats

What demotivates Barret?	Too much spontaneity—he likes plans, doesn't like when plans have to be changed, too much alone time, long-lasting tasks, too much inside time
What does Barret ask to do more than anything else?	Friend time and physical activities
What does Barret naturally do well?	Small tasks when asked, work with Dad
What does Barret need to work on?	Longer term projects, tasks, goals, daily routines like practicing his violin, and reading—not a fan

Some of Barret's incentives and their All Done Day coupon value:

Sleepover with a friend (at our house) – 7 All Done Day coupons
Sleepover with a friend (at their house) – 6 All Done Day coupons (less preparation/coordination on my part, so more easily awarded)
Movie and treats with a friend – 7 All Done Day coupons
Ice cream outing with Dad – 5 All Done Day coupons

What Motivates My Child?

It's very interesting to observe what Barret's passions and motivators are now that he is in his late twenties. He is still a morning person, he still loves spending time with friends, he is always willing to help someone, he loves being outside riding his motorcycle, and he still has a sweet tooth! (I am giving his wife this idea of creating a grown-up incentive list to help her when she needs to motivate him!)

What are Mitchell's passions?	Playing with Legos or video games (for hours if allowed) and playing soccer
What makes Mitchell happy?	Creating with Legos, reaching the next level on a video game, reading Calvin and Hobbes comic books, and food
What energizes Mitchell?	Figuring something out. Watching and reciting funny lines from TV and movies, laughing, and playing
What gets Mitchell up in the morning?	Not a morning person! The promise of his favorite cereal or knowing he had a soccer game that day helped get him up

What will Mitchell drop everything for?	Video games, Legos, going to a movie, snacks, or food
What demotivates Mitchell?	When someone does not believe in him and when he is interrupted
What does Mitchell ask to do?	Shop for a new Lego set, play video games, have a friend over to play Legos or video games, and spend time with Dad
What does Mitchell naturally do well without much pushing?	Not that much! Needs incentives! Content watching his brother clean their room. He does like working and playing with little kids when he serves in the church nursery.
What does Mitchell need to work on?	Following through when asked to do things and being more aware of life and people around him

Some of Mitchell's incentives and their All Done Day coupon value:

New small Lego set – 8 All Done Day coupons
Video game play date with 2-hour limit – 5 All Done Day coupons
Daddy Donut Date – 5 All Done Day coupons

We also encouraged Mitchell to work on developing his creative side and being with people through community theater. He landed some rewarding and memorable roles. Having mentors like the directors of his plays or soccer coaches in his life helped encourage him to make long-term goals, helped him learn to receive instruction and criticism, as well as affirmation.

Mitchell is now in his mid-twenties and he is developing into an adult who enjoys the challenge of problem solving in his graduate studies. Even though he enjoys the escape of an occasional video game, he is involved in friend groups and service projects. He still loves to recite movie lines and is very creative and witty in his Instagram posts.

Two great sons, same parents, different passions, and different motivators. Neither was better than the other, but they both needed personalized plans and incentives to help them to get from where they were to where they are today.

Just looking at these observations of our two sons, as in the exercise I outlined above, you can see that there were unique characteristics of each of our sons that in the course of an average day might be overlooked. When I realized what demotivated each of them, I was more sensitive to not aggravate them, and focus on how I could motivate and not exasperate them. I truly felt like I was understanding each of them better in the distinct ways that each of them needed to be loved. I felt like a better mom.

In addition to observing your child, be intentional about getting to know them. Make sure you ask your children lots of questions. For some of us (like me), this does not come easily, especially when busy family life was swallowing me up. But know that, with practice, you can get much better. Your kids will get used to sharing with you, and with time, you will enjoy mutual respect and will have earned the right to know what is going on inside them. You will continue to pick up more insight into what they value, what they fear, and what motivates them.

Chapter 8

The Building Blocks of Your Child's Daily Plan

After you have determined what motivates your child, the next step will be to start building their personalized daily plan by selecting appropriate tasks. Assigning tasks is not rocket science, but it needs to be done carefully. Consider each child individually, yet remember they are part of the greater family. Assigning age-appropriate and personality-compatible tasks is vital to the success of the plan!

For stepchildren who live in the home part time, they can and should be given a full All Done Day plan as well. The only difference is they can participate (and achieve awards) only when they are in your home. Don't let them off the hook and don't give them too much. Have confidence this will go well and help the other children understand that they can't compare their tasks with their siblings.

You can keep fine tuning the All Done Day plan, don't worry about doing it perfectly. The most important step is to START! Think of it as a soft launch but start just the same. If it is all in your head, and not on your children's doors or walls or on their screen notes, you will not make any progress.

Included at the end of this chapter are two types of All Done Day plan charts. You can select which one you want to use. One chart is pretty open, just fill in your child's plan. The other chart allows you to incorporate broader goals you want them to achieve.

Age-Appropriate or Ability-Level Tasks

When you choose tasks for your younger children, their plan might need to be made up of photos instead of words. Post a picture of their cleaned-up toy box or their folded clothes. They will love it if their plan is fun and colorful! You can even put them in the picture of the clean room with a big smile on their face or relaxing on their made bed with a book or listening to music! Clean rooms make moms and dads smile too!

When children are older, their plan should still be clearly defined. Post a written list of the clean room expectations. This will solve the "but you never told me…" excuses that pre-teens and teenagers try to give. I have included a list of tasks with age suggestions. These are just guidelines, but they are helpful for your first round of assigning tasks.

Whatever the method, it is SO important to equip each child for success in the tasks that you assign. Do you know that there are YouTube videos for almost everything? Here's an idea for just the right child. Have them create "How To" YouTube videos. You can post them as unlisted (only those with link can view it) and share the links with Grandma and Grandpa. Get them a duvet so they do not have to fuss with a top sheet when making their bed. Buy more hangers or hooks for the child who has trouble folding or keeping clothes folded. Do they know that picking up their room means that there are no longer any clothes on the floor, under the bed, or in the corners of the closet? Do you expect them to dust or bring their dirty clothes to the laundry room? Develop acceptable and realistic standards for what the clean room looks like. This will help them avoid the feeling that they can never please you, which is extremely demotivating.

If expectations are clear, success will not only be possible, it will be commonplace.

It is your role as a parent to call them up, to help them become more productive, more able human beings. You want them to become contributors and not just takers in your household, because that will speak to what kind of influence they can make at school and on the job.

Even at age two, children are able to start accomplishing some light jobs that can become great accomplishments with the appropriate praise. And how great to start teaching a work ethic at this young age! You may not even need to hand out All Done Day coupons for incentives. Two- to three-year-olds can be rewarded pretty easily, usually with words of praise and a cool little sticker. If you are starting All Done Day with your oldest child as a toddler, plan to grow into the incentive step of the plan. Study your children and begin to learn what those incentives might be for each of them. You will need those incentives to keep them working toward the goals you set for them when they are older.

Elementary-age children will likely need help in understanding how to complete their tasks. The first few weeks you will probably need to be right alongside them as they do their tasks, to guide, teach, encourage, and praise. After that it may just be a matter of reminding them. At this age, some start to be self-directed while others still need lots of guidance. Keep at it!

Parents of children with special needs, take heart. You might need to take extra care in selecting their tasks, but this can work for them as well. As a matter of fact, some of our children with special needs will function better on a daily basis with this improved effort toward greater structure and feeling of accomplishment. More on this in the chapter titled, "When One Size Does Not Fit All." Regardless of the child, If you miss the target in assigning tasks, be flexible and be willing to adjust.

Personality-Appropriate Tasks

In this life, we all need to learn to do things we don't love to do. However, if there is a task that is really demotivating to one of your children, you could pass it on to another child. For example, if your son gags when he has to clean the cat's litter box (this was my least favorite chore when I was growing up), you could have mercy and trade that out to another child or just do it yourself. However, learning how to clean one's room is NOT something you can give a pass on. It's too important of a skill and habit.

With multiple kids, you could pair one child with another for a task so that the stronger could help and teach the less experienced one. For example, my daughter, Lauren, is a natural in the kitchen. Pairing her with a less adept chef sibling to bake a batch of cookies was a win-win situation. As another example, you could choose a task like matching socks and assign this to a child who needs a simple job and will not get distracted or decide it's fun to throw the socks up on the ceiling fan.

With some tasks like straightening up their room, it doesn't matter if they get done at a certain time, but feeding or walking the dog needs to be done at more predictable times. Assigning this to a child who grasps the need to do a job in a timely manner would be wise and syncs with his or her personality strength.

Educational Tasks

It is a great idea to tie into the All Done Day plans tasks that teach important skills. At some point, each of your children will have regular homework assignments that can be included in their plan. Keep the expectation of learning and expanding themselves going all summer long if you can. For some kids, daily reading is not a chore, but for others, it really needs to be built into their routine. If they are taking music lessons or language lessons, there needs to be a task of daily work built into that discipline.

For the summer months, you could purchase *Summer Brain Quest Between Grades* workbooks that keep their skills sharp. We used these in addition to our All Done Day plan and actually paid them per page that they completed. My sister-in-law offered this to her second grader and had a hard time turning it off! What a great problem to have! Be creative with this.

Another type of teaching task could be for a pre-teen or teenager to plan and cook one meal a week. They will learn time management, how to navigate in the kitchen, how much a meal costs (if you include them in the grocery shopping), and what it feels like when someone doesn't love the meal. Learning to plan for and execute the meal can set them up for success when they do leave home. Plus, I found that my kids were much more grateful for the meal when it was not their turn to prepare the food.

It is wise to begin with a smaller number of tasks and add more as the kids are handling the list. You can find ways to praise them as you add a task to the list but be careful that they do not feel defeated if you need to take something off their list. Try to keep the list fairly short! Think about your own to-do lists, after all. If they are too long, you are not motivated to start them, or worse, you get in the habit of accepting an undone list each evening!

The following is a list of age-appropriate tasks that you can use to build your All Done Day plans for each of your children. The age categories are not hard and fast assignments by any means, but you can use them as a guide.

Age-Appropriate Tasks

Ages 2 to 3 (Do not expect perfection but encourage effort!)

- Pick up toys (have a specific place for them to go)

- Dust (a feather duster makes it fun)

- Make bed (just require pulling up the covers and putting the pillow in place)

- Put dirty clothes in basket or hamper

- Empty small wastebaskets

- Hang up jacket on a hook

- Help feed pets

- Help pick up magazines/books

- Wash hands before meals

Ages 4 to 5

- Dress self

- Make own bed (make it easy with a comforter or duvet)

- Clear dishes from table (use lightweight, unbreakable dishes)

- Set table (provide a picture of a place setting)

- Dust

- Water plants

- Sweep (smaller broom makes it easier)

- Put dirty clothes in basket or hamper

- Get the mail (if it is safe to do so)

- Match socks

- Put away clean clothes into drawers or on hangers

- Feed pets

- Book time (reading)

- Car custodian – keep back seats cleaned up

Ages 6 to 12

- Make own bed (make it easy with a comforter or duvet)

- Brush teeth/floss

- Comb hair

- Choose outfit for next day

- Feed, brush, or walk pets, clean cages, etc.

- Unload dishwasher

- Load dishwasher

- Clean bathroom

- Make school lunches (or finish the rest after mom or dad makes the sandwich)

- Take out trash

- Use washer and dryer

- Fold laundry

- Put laundry away

- Vacuum, sweep, or mop

- Strip and change bed linens

- Devotions (spiritual reading)

- Read for _____ minutes a day

- Read to a younger sibling or an elderly grandparent

- Practice instrument, language, etc.

- Exercise

- Clean windows or mirrors

- Finish homework

- Keep floor in room picked up

- Table or dresser tops are cleaned off

- ___ minutes on Khan Academy, Coursera, Ted-Ed, etc.

- Homework

- Yard work (weeding, digging dandelions, raking, mowing, etc.)

- Maintaining a good attitude

- No picking on brother/sister

- Kind words
- Say, "What can I do to help" to a family member one time each day

Ages 13 to 16

- Any of the above, and:
- A higher level of "cleaning the bathroom"
- Clean the kitchen
- Test smoke alarms 1x a month
- Set personal goals

Ages 16-18

- Any of the previous that are appropriate, and:
- Drive siblings to school or activities
- Meet their curfew
- Communicate with you about their day, their plans
- Cook one meal a week

- Do a grocery shopping run (when asked or at certain intervals)

- Set a budget and have them take a sibling clothes shopping

Setting Personal Goals

One of the most rewarding aspects of the All Done Day plan in our family's experience was the setting of personal goals. This made each child's plan personal to them and allowed for tailor-made goals. As parents, we examined each child and melded our desires for them with their own thoughts and personal goals. We settled on these categories: Physical, Spiritual, Social, Academic, and Service. These were important to us parents, and we wanted to find goals for each child that would allow them to develop in these areas. We selected tasks or projects for each child and they often helped in choosing the projects.

Here are some examples of some of the goals we set for our children:

Physical – One of our daughters was more prone to spending her time reading and being inactive. We set a goal of getting outside and engaging in physical activity every day. This usually took the form of riding her bike, walking the dog, or playing soccer in the backyard with her siblings.

Spiritual – This was a family value that we wanted to promote, so we included a daily goal of having what we called a "devotional time." It was a block of time to read a spiritually focused book or have a time of personal prayer. Our children benefitted from this time that was quiet, introspective, and we believe it gave all of us more peace.

Social – This may be very helpful for a child who tends to be overly introverted or for a child who has a preoccupation with his/her phone or device. You may include in the plan a period of time each day that they leave their phone or device in a certain place to encourage reading, or even rest. If your child needs to be cultivating relationships, you could set a goal of having them invite a friend over once a week or make a new friend at lunch and eventually have that friend over to the house. Perhaps an appropriate social goal is to have that child call a friend instead of texting. Some might need help choosing a better friend group, and you could think of ways to address this in your goal setting. Step in, evaluate, and set goals that will help your child for the long haul.

Academic – This could simply be the task of completing daily homework assignments, or it could be a special goal for a child of striving for a "B" in a difficult class where they are currently doing "C" work. If you have a child who struggles to read, you may set a goal of reading fifteen minutes per day. Some goals are short-term, such as learning multiplication facts. If a high school student is preparing for AP exams, they could have a goal of working on memorizing terms or working sample math problems for twenty minutes a day. Another idea for an academic goal could be for a child to build their vocabulary by learning a new word each day, and at the dinner table, they will be expected to share that new word and use it in a sentence.

Service – One of our family values is to care for others. There are so many ways to nurture this, but even more than the other categories, it does not happen on its own. Children need to see this modeled and they need opportunities to practice. We had elderly neighbors who lived next door. We let our children know that any time it snowed, they were expected to help us shovel our neighbor's driveway in addition to ours. Our kids developed an unexpected, sweet connection with this couple which gave our kids a feeling of being needed. If service assignments are irregular, like whenever it snows, you could award an extra All Done Day coupon for that task in addition to their daily plan.

A great benefit of making the All Done Day plan part of your child's routine is that you can insert plan items that develop specific character traits. This also gives you the opportunity to tie their personalized plan to your family values or targets.

As you get to know your children in a deeper way, it will be more evident which traits are more natural to them and which traits need to be nurtured. It is so helpful to have a plan to have them working on these things.

Below are some examples of character traits and then teaching tasks or measures that you can insert into their daily plan. It is good to switch these up to keep them on their toes, and to nurture more great character qualities in your kids. As you do so, their strengths and weaknesses will become evident. Everyone can learn to be kind, trustworthy, persistent, and so on.

Character Trait	**Teaching Tasks/ Measurements**
Integrity/Honesty/ Trustworthiness	Have your child's coupon award tied to truthfulness in completing daily plan or telling the truth throughout their day
Self-control	Not provoking siblings No tantrums No whining—talk to us with a reasonable voice
Self-discipline	Work your plan Don't procrastinate

The Building Blocks of Your Child's Daily Plan

Kindness	Get caught being kind
Have an "others first" attitude
Daily offer to "help others"
Generosity	Look for ways to share (big or small)
Personal giving (\$ from allowance or savings)
Service Projects (big or small)
Persistence	Work toward a specific goal: learn times table, shoot for an athletic PR (personal record), memorize a part for a play, a poem, a Bible verse, or a music piece
Positivity/Optimism	Use "upper" statements in place of "downer" statements. Don't grumble.
Gratitude/Appreciation	Make "thank-you" part of your DNA. Even more than words, (but the words are a good start), actions of gratitude. An example

	would be helping to clear the table for a meal served to you.
Personal Health	Choose healthy snacks Daily physical activity Go to bed by _____ each night

Note: The following All Done Day plan forms can be accessed by downloading them at alldoneday.com/forms.

ALL DONE DAY PLAN

Name:

An All Done Day for ME consists of:

-
-
-
-
-
-

YOU CAN DO IT!

ALL DONE DAY PLAN

Name:

An All Done Day for ME consists of:

-

-

-

-

-

-

Personal Goals:

Physical –

Spiritual –

Social –

Service –

Academic –

Chapter 9

An Important Element of the All Done Day Plan:Creating Incentives and Rewards

In Chapter 7 we discussed ways to determine what motivates your child, and we touched on how important the incentive piece of the All Done Day plan became. Because of their importance and because I want to help you to get this right, I want to give you more direction. The most important element of making All Done Day successful for your children is to create incentives that are truly motivating—and yes—FUN for them. This is the big prize at the finish line. "What's in it for me?" is naturally the big question, and because of your planning sessions, you will have a great answer!

We all need goals to shoot for, targets to aim at, and that is what the incentives provide. They pull us along and drive us to the finish line. The beauty of creative incentives is that they can work in your budget. You don't have to spend a lot of money to reward your children. As a matter of fact, sometimes the most expensive awards don't really have the value that you think they should. Instead, plan on spending more TIME, INVOLVE-MENT, and CREATIVITY. Any parent that invests these three things will always create memories and have better relationships with their children. I found that many of the incentives that my children worked the hardest for involved time alone with Mom or Dad.

Probably the trickiest task is to assign a value to the incentive. An example would be: 1 Friend sleepover at my house = 7 All Done Day coupons. Make some incentives easy to earn and purposely design some to be "reaches" that require saving. Those are enjoyed because of the anticipation and the journey to get there. Be careful to avoid "demotivating" by setting the goal too high. On the other hand, you don't want a steady stream of rewards with no effort. No one can decide this better than you because of how well you know your child.

Don't compare one child to another, and work hard to find balance between being realistic and too-high expectations. I have purposely refrained from giving you numeric coupon values for the incentives because this is such a subjective exercise and must fit the needs of your own child. Be sure to let your children know that there will be adjustments in the plan as you go and that it's nothing personal, just a process for everyone to learn.

Be firm.

Kids DO need and secretly value rules!

(Have you ever played board games together? The rules are a big part of the fun!) If you set up an incentive for sleepovers and then allow them a sleepover without making them spend their coupons, you have just torpedoed your whole system. If the child wants to be ready to be able to say "yes" to a spur of-the-moment sleepover invitation, then explain to them that they may be wise to build up coupons so they would be ready should that situation arise. This teaches saving, planning, and spending. Possibly the greatest motivator for a child could be missing a sleepover because they did not have enough coupons saved up to buy the incentive.

You can also teach them about concepts of saving. If you help them realize that it would be a good idea to have a reserve of All Done Day coupons available so that if a sleepover opportunity came up unexpectedly, they would be prepared. This is a real-life type of scenario that teaches money and resource management. If you have several children, you are certain to have some "savers" and some "quick spenders." They can learn from each other and from disappointments. Be courageously firm when they are caught without resources. They may be very unhappy at first, but they will remember that pain and hopefully choose to create a coupon reserve going forward.

When you select the incentives that you decide to offer your children, write them down and assign a point redemption value to each one. Post these somewhere or keep in a folder that they can access. Don't be afraid to adjust the incentives or values at any time and communicate and explain any changes clearly with your children. Surprises are not fair.

Remember, YOU are the administrator, the teacher, AND the PARENT! Some aspects of life are NOT negotiable, and you are the one setting the rules. But having reasons and explanations will prove that you are very involved in the plan, and also care about their growth and happiness.

I have provided a very short list of incentives.

Incentives List

Daddy Donut Date

Art/Craft Project Night

1 Sleepover at home with 1 Friend

Thrifting Trip Date

No Chore Day of Choice

Movie & Popcorn

Hike

Bike Ride (with treat)

Home Pedicure/Manicure

One Extra Bedtime Story

Build an Outdoor or Indoor Obstacle Course

Extra Time on Device

Trip to _____

Chapter 10

Planning Session

The All Done Day plan takes some planning, but this book provides many tools to make it easy and fun! Your best successes come because you put thought into customizing your day-to-day use of the plan.

To get ready for your planning session:

- If you are a two-parent home or a blended family, ensure participation of you and your spouse.

- If you are a single parent or a single guardian, enlist the help of a close friend or family member who knows your children, their personalities and strengths, and will be a support when you need a pep talk.

- Pick a location where you can talk, whether that is a coffee shop, the kitchen table, or an evening phone call.

- Have a pencil with eraser or a computer. You WILL be making changes as you go.

- Put on an adventurous spirit. You are trying something new and have every good reason to be optimistic!

Work on one child at a time to devise the task lists. You will want to keep the other children in mind if you are filling in tasks that are affecting others, like rotating the bathroom cleaning and vacuuming, for example.

When you are on the first launch of All Done Day, it's important to start small. Assign fewer tasks to see how your child handles them. Always be ready to adjust your list if it needs to be adjusted.

Make sure you include everyone! Even the smallest members of your home can handle responsibility and will gladly hold you accountable! They will watch to see if you are buying into this and achieving your own All Done Day! Be sure to create some of your own tasks and incentives as your children are watching you too.

Imagine how you could
justify an uninterrupted bubble bath
or a trip to the driving range simply
because YOU EARNED IT!

Print off these forms (available on
www.alldoneday.com/forms)

- All Done Day Plan (one per child)

- Incentives Worksheet

- All Done Day Coupons

- Grace Coupons

Here is How We Built Our Plan

1. We sat down and determined what our top family values or "targets" were going to be. Yours will likely be different, but here was our list:

- Develop good work ethic – through daily household tasks

- Develop love for music/arts – through music

lessons, listening, and attending concerts and plays

- Become lifelong learners – through reading, experiences

- Serve others – through family and community outreach opportunities

- Develop spiritually – through church and personal devotions

2. Choose a child and determine what motivates him/her.

(Ten-Year-Old Lauren's motivators)

Feeling "special"

Positive words, encouragement

Meeting a goal

Alone time with Mom or Dad

Getting time to read

Anything to do with horses

3. Choose incentives that will work for that child.

(Ten-Year-Old Lauren's Incentives)

Daddy donut date

Craft time with Mom

A special type of collectible stuffed animal

A DQ Blizzard or frozen yogurt date

Anything to do with horses (See a horse movie, a horse series book, or a plastic Breyer horse or accessory)

Pick out a new book

4. Make out a daily All Done Day Plan for each child. (Lauren's example continues) Be sure to choose age and personality-appropriate tasks.

- Make bed

- Clean floor in bedroom (dirty clothes in laundry basket, toys and books put away)

- Empty dishwasher (as needed—so CHECK!)

- Exercise (ride bike, take a walk, run, or play with sibs)

- Daily prayer time

5. Implement the plan and watch the magic happen!

Sample All Done Day Plans

Here are some examples of plans that our kids actually used. For a fun comparison, I am showing the plans for all four of our children, at two different ages. The first is a plan from when they were younger. The second is a plan they created for themselves when they were in their high school and college years!

Barret (8 years old)

Make bed
Pick up/straighten room
Reading or workbook time (20 min.)
Practice instrument(s)
Devotions
Exercise
Water flowers

Barret (20 years old)

Morning Devotions
Work (he had a job)
Physical Work Out
Complete a summer reading list
Practice violin 3x a week

Lauren (11 years old)

Make bed
Pick up/straighten room
Reading and exercise (alternate days)
Practice instrument
Set table for dinner
Devotions

Lauren (21 years old)

Work out (goal – to run a 5K)
Devotions (write in journal)
Work (job)
Practice piano (learn a sonatina)
Study for GRE (grad school)
Service – Help w/children's church

Mitchell (5 years old)

Make bed
Pick up toys
Devotions
Workbook time (15 min)
Car custodian (keep back seat clean)

Mitchell (16 years old)

Soccer workout (timed)
Running and 200 soccer ball touches a day
Work (job)
Devotions
Practice trumpet
Service (church nursery and tutoring at the trailer park after school)

Megan (3 years old)

Make bed
Pick up toys
Put dirty clothes in basket
Wash hands before meals

Megan (14 years old)

Clean room
Practice piano/violin/clarinet
Summer reading list
Soccer workout (running/touches)
Service (church nursery/babysitting)
Work (part-time job)

Chapter 11

Record Keeping
and Reward Day

All Done Day will fall apart quickly if there is no management. So, an adult or trusted person needs to be the "All Done Day Coupon Keeper." He or she will have to check up daily on the All Done Day participants. Don't just rely on memory. DO check up on your kids to make sure they are completing their WHOLE plan. A former CEO of IBM Corporation, Louis V. Gerstner, Jr., wisely said, "People don't do what you expect, but what you inspect." Checking up on your kids' All Done Day progress will need to become part of your routine.

How you award the coupons will be up to you. It's often timely to present the coupon for the achieved All Done Day at bedtime each day. This acknowledges the achievement, gives a natural opportunity for daily praise, and makes certain that you don't forget to award your child. I know that if I had not awarded coupons daily, I would have lost track of the completed versus the not completed days. And anarchy would have taken over.

Creating a daily routine of checking in with your kids will also give you the opportunity to tell them you are sorry when they do NOT finish their tasks and that they will have a new chance tomorrow to achieve an All Done Day. Remember, try not to communicate condemnation, just stick with reality and show little to no emotion. Do not ever chide them or say things to make them feel bad. With this new system in place, you shouldn't need to do that. You can, however, come alongside them by saying, "I am sorry you didn't finish your list, but let's keep our head up and get it done tomorrow. I know you can do it." This is a valuable technique to learn because it prevents you from demeaning your child. Be empathetic but be firm. Resist the urge to cave in, and don't give them a coupon just because they came close or are protesting your decision.

Having all your kids on the All Done Day plan will create built-in accountability and peer pressure that you could not ever engineer on your own. Because of different personality types, you may have some kids complete their plan in the morning because that's just the way they roll. And then there are the last-minute types that rush to get it done right before bedtime and coupon time. (I had both.) But more often than not, they develop an awareness of each other and seem to even each other out. We found the compulsive child mellowed and spread the daily tasks out a bit, and the last-minute child learned some lessons on getting things done earlier and avoiding last-minute stress.

Sometimes it can be a bit of a challenge if two kids share a room and have different levels of urgency in getting their room cleaned. Remember the reality that they will need to work with all types of people throughout their lives, and you can help the siblings learn ways to work together now. Foster family encouragement. Everyone wants to enjoy their earned incentives. If one child is repeatedly struggling to finish their plan, enlist the whole family to cheer them on and offer encouragement. But do not do their work for them!

Schedule a Reward Day on a family calendar so your kids know when the incentives will be given out. They will know to save up the coupons for the incentives some time before Reward Day. Be sure to hold your commitment and really celebrate Reward Day! Consider picking out a great celebration song that becomes your anthem! This is the pinnacle of the entire All Done Day plan and everything they are learning through it.

This Reward Day, however, does not have to be the only time you allow a child to redeem their coupons for a reward. For example, if an invitation for a sleepover would come up quickly and they have enough coupons to "buy" it, you could let them cash in and enjoy their earned reward.

Be sure to keep track of what your child "buys" as an incentive in case it's something they can't cash in on immediately. There will be instances when a reward has to be scheduled, like when they choose a Dad or Mom date.

A word of caution: don't keep the All Done Day coupons where they can be taken without permission. When the incentives are well planned, temptation will be there to get to the goal by any means possible. The coupons have room to write the child's name or initials, so they are not transferable between siblings. You could also initial or write a personal note on the back. These have to be earned, people! Another way you can keep each child's coupons separate is to print them out on different colors of paper.

The Place for Grace

Grace is getting something we do not deserve. We all need it from time to time. We need to receive it and we need to give it. There will be days when your kids will be sick or overly tired. There are days when their world is just so chaotic that an All Done Day will be unrealistic. This is totally a judgement call by the parent. There will be days when they didn't make it happen and they won't get the coupon. In our home, we used Grace Coupons very sparingly, but they were extremely nice to have.

Even before we instituted the All Done Day plan in our family, we were incorporating incentives and grace into our kids' days. My oldest daughter participated in a 100-day piano practice challenge. If she achieved the 100 days in a row, she would receive a trophy from her piano teacher. She had bought into the challenge, and it was reaping great benefits in the progress she was making in her proficiency at the keyboard. On one extremely hectic day of soccer games, she was totally worn out. She got home late in the evening and did not have anything left in her tank. We made a judgement call to give our daughter grace for that day and would require her to practice two times the next day. (Her piano teacher approved of this plan.) This made a big impression on my daughter. It wasn't that she got out of something, but that she was allowed to still reach her goal when her circumstances seemed impossible.

*Just as parents can be too loose
on rules, parents can also be too strict
on rules, and it can injure a child's heart.*

The Grace Coupons help parents extend grace, and they do make an impression. My daughter remembers this situation twenty years later!

Chapter 12

Kicking Off Your
All Done Day Adventure!

All Done Day is an adventure that your whole family is going to go on together, and you will reap benefits as a family as well as individually! Consider launching All Done Day with a family meeting that is as fun as a grand opening celebration is for a business. Include a fun activity and a treat everyone will enjoy. The more positive you are from the start, the more likely you will have buy-in from everyone in the family.

Be ready for some groans and some resistance, especially from your teenagers, but do not give in! Children will not choose accountability on their own, but they will work for the rewards! Be the cheerleader and keep them at this until they realize how much they will benefit from it, both now and in the long term.

A great time to begin All Done Day is either at the start of summer break or when school is beginning in the Fall. Some families have found success starting it in January as well. With a change in routine, it is a good time to spur discipline and create accountability.

Ideas for the Kick-Off Meeting

Treasure Hunt*
Scavenger Hunt
Bowling Night
Game Night
Blindfolded Dinner
Ice Cream for Dinner
Dinner and a Movie with a Theme
Create a special video

*Sample Treasure Hunt

Create some suspense. Let your children know that when they have finished their meal, there is going to be a special surprise! If they are older, and have phones, send a text during the day that will create some anticipation. You will have to prepare a special dessert or treat, plant the clues, and have your All Done Day task and incentive lists prepared to present to the family.

The first clue could be taped to the bottom of their dinner plate. If you have several children, you could put a part of the clue under each one's plate so that they have to work together. When the meal is wrapping up, tell them they must go together to find each clue. No running ahead of a younger sibling!

Clue 1:
(In an envelope that the oldest—or only child—opens and reads)

Hurry, Hurry, Don't Be Late

There's Something Under Your Dinner Plate!

Clue 2:
(Under Dinner Plate)

Do Not Stop to Take a Drink

Your Next Clue is By the Sink!

Clue 3:
(Near Sink)

No, No, No It's Not Time for Bed

But Go and Look Where You Lay Your Head

Clue 4:
(On Pillow)

> You Are Getting Closer, and You are A Winner
>
> Where is the Place Where We Cook Dinner?

Clue 5:
(Stove/Microwave)

> Whether You are Girls or You are Boys,
>
> Your Next Clue is With Your Toys!

Clue 6:
(Toy Box)

> You are GREAT, You are SWEET
>
> Come Back to the Table for a Special Treat!

At the dinner table, have a special treat set out. Explain the All Done Day Adventure that will start TOMORROW!

Chapter 13

When One Size Doesn't Fit All

Moms of children with special needs are so remarkable to me. I've been around many of these amazing parents, and in my estimation, they are parenting at a whole new level. Each one I talked to in preparation for writing this book is a student of their child and seems to be further along than most of us in determining what motivates their child. Their advice was practical for any parent, so stick with me and we'll learn together!

Many thanks to Mary, Janelle, Amy, Sarah, Rebecca, and Kim, for their vulnerability and willingness to give me a window into the unique challenges of raising a child with Downs Syndrome, Autism, ADHD, BiPolar, Anxiety and Separation Issues, and Pataki-Lupski Syndrome (PLS). Across the board, every single mom stressed the need for routine and consistency in their homes. This gives children a sense of security and direction. Spontaneity for some of these children is threatening and routines like All

Done Day can help cut down on feelings of chaos. Sarah agreed wholeheartedly with this assessment.

Another common thread in our conversations was that children with special needs usually require help and supervision to complete tasks. Mary told me that with her daughter, chores get divided into categories of "I Do," "We Do," and "You Do." Realistic expectations are SO important in reducing frustration for the parent and the child. The goal needs to be tied to what your child is capable of doing rather than what is standard among typical children. Parents of kids with special needs understand this completely, in large part because they usually have other children who do not have learning or behavior difficulties.

Rebecca felt it was vital to tailor jobs to match their abilities. Her five-year-old daughter can fold laundry well but her six-and-a-half-year-old son cannot due to some motor skill issues. He is, however, successful in delivering laundry baskets of clean clothes to rooms, and enthusiastically changes toilet paper rolls whenever needed. Those jobs empower him. "In our home we focus on 'THIS is what you can contribute,'" Rebecca said.

Janelle explained, "Chores must be very specific. Not just 'clean up your room,' but every detail needs to be spelled out." This was accomplished with using pictures when her son was younger, and now he can read a list. She did the chores in tandem with him until he understood the expectations.

There needs to be a balance of appropriate expectations and a realistic perspective on success. Amy pointed out, "Who cares if she breaks a plate—she is setting the table! Who cares if she used too much jelly—she is making her own sandwich!" She also pointed out that children with special needs are almost always in a position of being helped in some way because of their limitations. They receive help at school, at therapy, in public, and at home. When they DO get the chance to do something for someone else, they tend to walk taller.

Being the helper rather than the
one who is being helped is a big deal.
We can help make that happen!

There are times to "try out some chores" to see if your child is able to accomplish a task. Amy found that after returning home from being away for a week, her daughter had taken care of some tasks she hadn't been expecting her to do. Finding appropriate, manageable tasks is one of the ongoing necessary jobs for parents in this process. All children develop and mature to some level. To continually meet them where they are at is part of the All

Done Day strategy. Our parents of special needs are shining examples of this!

The team mentality that comes from a family working toward an All Done Day is motivating. When "everyone is doing it," even the most reluctant participants can be encouraged to succeed. Positive competition turns into camaraderie. Don't forget to give your children the right to check up on YOU. Let them see you working through your own list. Don't be afraid to let them see a day where you don't make it.

Incentives are key to an All Done Day, but you may need to adjust for a child with special needs. Incentives may not be as effective in motivating children who lack the cognitive skills to connect the task completion to the reward. So again, parents need to be trying things out to see what works and what does not work. One size does NOT always fit all. Rebecca tied things up nicely as she pointed out that, "It is important to see that your children are involved in the process, and that the process is getting better."

As I spent time with these moms who carry a lot on their shoulders and their hearts, I was struck by the realization that not one of them ever complained. They were truly determined to be the parents that each of their children needed. That is the best any of us can do!

Chapter 14

Involving Your Children

As much as you are the parent and project manager of this All Done Day venture, you can and should involve your kids in the process. First of all, gaining "buy-in" is a must. If your children are still pretty small, they worship the ground you walk on, and any new idea presented with "fun" will fly. But as your kids get older and wiser to the world, they are going to be more critical. Because of this, you cannot just throw this together. They will be able to tell if you have not embraced the plan yourself. So, the more thought you put into how you introduce it and how you will communicate expectations and encouragement from day to day, the greater success you will achieve.

With older children, you can have them help you come up with their daily plan. Give them the blank All Done Day form and see where they go with it. At first, don't give a lot of direction so you can see what they would define as an All Done Day. Make sure they know that their plan will be reviewed, and together you'll make sure it's a good list. Encourage them to take this seriously. They may do a better job than you would imagine! You might even pencil in a plan for them on your own, so you have thought through it before you meet together. Remember, anything is negotiable, within reason.

In this meeting time, you can use this time to talk about tasks that need to be done but are not popular. Discourage them from monitoring a sibling's work. Stress the importance of owning their own plan; their own daily success. Encourage long-term goals and help them see that a good work ethic will make them valuable employees someday. And in the present, they can be valuable students, team members, and friends.

There are so many benefits to be gained, and they will outweigh the work that has to be done to get there. No one really *loves* to make their bed, but they will see how nice it feels to have a task completed before leaving their bedroom in the morning! Offer real examples about times in your life when you were given more responsibility because your hard work was recognized. Or perhaps tell them about times when you realized that you were passed over because you were just "getting by" and not exhibiting extra effort. These conversations can add fuel to the All Done Day program and they will see that effort really does make a big difference.

Chapter 15

Working with Teenagers

There are definitely considerations to be made when you are starting the All Done Day plan with teenagers. First of all, you will be working against habits that have been set for quite a while, and there can be significant resistance.

I can imagine that parents who are starting this when their child is a teenager are doing it because they are seeing areas of their child's life that are lacking and want to help them to develop those areas. You are realizing that the time they have under your care and training is limited and you are feeling a sense of urgency to instill good habits in them. You are a bold and loving parent! Don't give up! Your efforts are such a gift to your children! It will be worth everything you and they put into this. You will be amazed when they begin to "own" their list and start to be self-propelled in order to earn the rewards.

Be ready to defend any tasks you propose that they might question. Anticipate their pushback and be ready to explain your reasons for inserting the All Done Day plan in their routine. "Because I said so" will not cut it. You might need to explain how being organized in a certain area can help them find order in other parts of their life. Having a daily practice schedule for their instrument, for example, will help them to ensure the daily discipline and help meet other goals that may be set by a music instructor. Look at life skills that are important for them to have by the time they leave home, and the ones they are not proficient in; add to their daily plan, switching them out as they master each one.

To help your teen realize that you are not just dumping this on them, it would be a good idea for you to make your own All Done Day plan and have them see you working through it. Be sure to include some tasks that you really do not like to do. Also think of some life skills you may not have mastered that you can put on your list. If you do this, every family member will be working toward something, and it will give your household a different atmosphere; a sense of forward action and completion.

Have your teen set some of their own personal goals. This helps them to not drift. It can help them grow and explore other areas of interest. Teens sometimes flounder but setting goals and having a plan will help them stay focused and achieve their goals.

After many years of using the All Done Day plan with our children, we did not always rely on the daily incentives to motivate completion of their task list. It was more of a family expectation and because we had our teenagers compile lists that we approved, they had ownership and buy-in and were more invested in completion. We still encouraged them and would remind them at times, but it was not as much of a daily checkup as it was a weekly check-in to see how they were doing.

We chose at times to reward the completion of a personal goal, like a special celebratory dinner after Megan participated in a Sonatina Festival, following months of practice and preparation. We lavished over-the-top praise and admiration when our son and daughter passed the "speed test" of their soccer try-out because of their daily task of running that they had set for themselves. My sister Barb's family plan one summer was a "boot camp" to keep their boys physically active in the summer. When they achieved certain levels, there was a family outing for malts at a popular ice cream shop. Rewards will vary with your child and their specific motivators.

You will want to identify your negotiables when they are setting their own task lists. Maybe Mom wants to have the teen work on making their bed daily, but the clean room is a once-a-week expectation and will have to pass an inspection. If the bed is not being made daily, ask them what might help them meet their goal. They may need incentives, and they can be helpful in setting what those incentives should be.

It is a good feeling to meet a goal, but even adults need tangible rewards at times to get us to change a behavior or meet a deadline!

Be sure to use screen time as an incentive. It is a privilege and a responsibility that requires discipline and oversight. If teens are allowed unlimited use of screens, having an All Done Day will be put at the bottom of their priority list. They want to have screen time, so tie it to the reward of finishing their daily plan. You may have a statement at the top of their plan list that outlines this requirement. Example: "Approved screen time must follow the completion of the listed items." Grumbling can be met with a non-emotional reminder of how they can achieve screen time.

You are trying to teach your kids how to focus on getting important things done. It is your job to help them know when to put the devices down and get things done. Screens used irresponsibly or without self-control can take them away from things that are more important. They need to build good habits and resolve to be able to say "no" to less worthwhile things in order to say "yes" to better things. You may require that homework and certain items in their All Done Day plan be complete before they have approved screen time. This can be an immediate reward for meeting expected daily goals. If you work it into the plan, you will not have to nag or scold. Lay out the expectations and stand firm. The outcome of their choices will be up to them. You will have to follow through, though. You may have to have phones checked in to you or dropped in a basket until they have met the criteria for earning the time. Enforcement is essential; even some adults have trouble self-monitoring their screen time!

I think if I were implementing the All Done Day plan for the first time when my kids were teens, I would have approached the parents of some of my kids' friends to see if they would participate too, so there would be some solidarity in my efforts. It is so common for your teens to say, "But none of my friends have to do this!" Take away the opportunity for them to talk like this. Just think of the idea sharing that could happen if parents talked about incentives and ideas for helping their teens set personal goals.

Don't be afraid to tap into the resources around you. With our search engines always at our fingertips, we can tend to search for answers on our own and are not building and depending upon communities that can help us and encourage us. Bring the All Done Day plan to your "tribe" and see how you can learn and grow together.

I can envision a coach presenting the All Done Day plan to the parents of their athletes as a way to take the discipline beyond the field, the court, or the pool. Busy teens can accomplish so much more when they have a plan!

Teens will probably appreciate their plan lists being in their notes app on their phones rather than a list posted on their door. Give them dignity and use the mode of communication or record keeping that works best for them. Make the incentives worthwhile and watch them succeed!

Chapter 16

Tools for Encouragement

You have a great opportunity to pour life into your kids as you respond to them achieving their All Done Days. This may seem obvious, but it is so easy to forget to build other people up.

We love it when others compliment us; it feeds us in ways that are hard to even verbalize.

Some of us did not grow up in positive environments, so we must learn how to be generous with our words. You will never be sorry you did!

In our family, we have intentionally inserted traditions that help teach our children the importance of encouragement. At birthday dinners, we go around the table and share affirmation for the birthday boy or girl, and this has continued into adulthood. It was especially touching to hear that our new daughter-in-law, Lauren Marie, took this into one of her extended family gatherings. I love seeing the birthday guy or gal be a little embarrassed at the beginning and completely flattered by the end. It takes the focus off the gifts or food and places it on the special person you are celebrating.

Leadership mentor Michael Hyatt says, "Our words carry enormous weight. More than we sometimes think. They often impact people for decades, providing the courage to press on or one more reason not to give up."[4] A person who feels appreciated will almost always achieve more than is expected. Personally, when I am praised and built up, it fuels me to try harder, to do more. Why wouldn't I try doing that for my kids?

Here are some great phrases to store in your quiver of praise for lifting up your children:

Way to go!
You are amazing!
I really appreciate what you did!
You are a champion!
You did it!
You did it again!

---

[4] "How Our Words Impact Others" michaelhyatt.com

I love watching you play!
Boom!
Score!
That makes me smile!
Well done!
Your effort blows me away!
Thank you for caring!
Wow!
Bravo!
You make me smile!
Give me five!
Good for you!
Super!
Fantastic!
Take a bow!
Great stuff!
Amazing!
I am impressed!
Great job!
Superb!
Fabulous!
Congratulations!
You rocked it!
Right on!
You did that yourself!
You sure make this family great!
You should feel proud!

All Done Day

Pat yourself on the back!
I am SO proud of you!
YOU can be proud of YOURSELF!
You are a star!
I think you are fantastic!
Great job!
You are a great example!
You did that so well!
That shows self-discipline!
Success!
That really made a difference!
You are THE BEST!
I admire your hard work!
Awesome!
You're one in a million!
You are making this world a better place!
I can rely on you!
You are going places!

With younger children, it can be fun to make up a family cheer/chant. Here are a few examples:

Hey, Hey, Hey, it's an All Done Day!

If you ask us we can say, _____ loves an All Done Day!

I don't care what they may say, _____'s got an All Done Day!

You can look for positive words that start with the first letter of your child's name. Check out www.adjectivesstarting.com for ideas. Someone has done the work for you! So, if my child's name is Megan, I might find these words to help me make positive statements:

Magnificent Megan!

Megan—that was Major League!

Megalithic! (A large stone or monument)

Megascopic! (Visible to the naked eye—make THEM look it up. It doesn't have to make sense when it sounds awesome and you deliver it that way)

Positive words are memorable and can fuel perseverance in the journey toward meeting the goals you have set for your children. Go fill them up!

Chapter 17

Changing the Rules

As much as routine can give us some direction and security, it can also become boring and eventually demotivating. So, it is important to be ready to insert some surprises or ways to change things up to keep everyone engaged. Here are some ways to make the All Done Day plan unpredictable and fresh:

- **Double Coupon Day or Week** – Have a place in your home where everyone can watch for All Done Day "special offers." Giving a time period of extra coupons can breathe some new life into those who are working for a special reward, or for those who have been lagging in their commitment.

- **Mystery Days** – Have an All Done Day Calendar you buy at the Dollar Store and on different days, create fun rewards. Maybe you will write "Dad will make your bed today!" or this can be how you post the "Double Coupon Day." You could cover that "prize" with some blue painter's tape so there can be a "reveal" that morning. Make a rule that there is NO PEEKING before the day, and if they forget to look on the day, they forfeit the prize. Maybe create extra task opportunities that allow a child the ability to gain a reward sooner. You could offer an extra coupon to everyone if the family needs to pull together to get the house ready quickly for company. This teaches teamwork and is an excellent training ground for those who like to "keep track" of someone else's work progress. If the team gets the house clean, every player gets a coupon. Part of earning that extra coupon could be doing the work without any grumbling! There is always room to be creative within your All Done Day plan!

- **Periodic Review** – Have a family meeting (great to do over ice cream sundaes or a favorite family treat) and rework your incentives/rewards with input from your users! This helps you to hear more of what motivates each of your children.

Parting Words for Parents

Just in case you have any lingering doubt, I want to assure you that this works! Instituting the All Done Day plan in your home will reap numerous benefits. You will be able to change from pushing your children to directing and guiding them. I was in a store recently and overheard a mother on the phone with her child, asking him if he had cleaned his room and the bathroom, and "just how clean is it?" That phone call would not even need to happen if the tasks and expectations had been laid out in an All Done Day plan.

One of the greatest perks to this system is that you will get to know your children like you have not known them before.

You will see new potential in them as they begin to experience success on a daily basis! And you will see their confidence grow as they acquire a new sense of purpose and discipline. They will begin to "own" their plan, and they will surely have fun enjoying the rewards that they earned!

Share Your All Done Day Story

Parents around the globe are so hungry for real life stories to give them ideas, encouragement, and fuel for their journey. You are warmly invited to share what worked for your family's All Done Day adventure by sending an email to stories@alldoneday.com.

Free Gift for You!

I am so glad you have a copy of *All Done Day: How to Win at Everyday Parenting*. Although crafting this plan taught me so much, I wish it had been available to me when my children were small, and I needed it most. To get you started, I am offering you free access to our basic All Done Day forms designed to make your launch easier. You will access the forms at www.AllDoneDay.com/forms.

Acknowledgements

Steve – I have been blessed a thousand-fold by your love, commitment, perseverance, and wisdom as my husband and parenting partner. This book would still just be "the good ideas that worked for our family" without your vision and encouragement. Je t'adore!

My Children – You were the world's best test subjects! Lauren, Barret, Mitchell, and Megan, you lived the plan and helped us refine it. Always remember the satisfaction of achieving an All Done Day!

Heidi Sheard – I am so thankful for how our paths reconnected through Facebook after having no contact for two decades! You were ruthless but kind. I am grateful and have learned so much. Your experience as a mom was key in the ways that you were able to ask for "more." I hope you enjoy more "All Done" editing days on new projects with me!

Scott Dvorak/Robyn Bernd of Balance Design – I was so afraid to look at your proposed designs. What if I hated them?

How do I let my friend down gently? Not to worry, I was floored. You hit a home run, fulfilling my wish list. It felt so gratifying to hear that you loved working on this project.

Sonja Carlson – You are my friend for life and author of so many mom ideas. Keep passing them on!

Judy Kline and Jane Jacobsen – You two asked me "How is the book going?" at just the right times to build me up or to kick me back into gear. I hope I can give back somehow.

Ryan and Stacy Lahm – You were great Beta testers. You launched *All Done Day* and proved what we knew to be true. (It works). Love you and love your kids!

Chandler Bolt and the Self-Publishing School Support Community – I hear your voice in my head: "Just write the dang book!" Okay – I DID!

My Launch Team – I am humbled for the many who took on "one more thing" to encourage and spur this project on. Just think, you will be able to say you were in on the beginning of the All Done Day tidal wave!

God – Thanks for the not-so-subtle nudge to get this project out of my files and into the hands of parents that need ideas that work. Following you is anything but boring.

About the Author

Ann Lahm (rhymes with "mom") is the mother of four grown and flown children. They are the reason for her smile lines and her gray hairs. Ann has worked in the corporate world as a contract administrator, and also worked as a private music educator and motivator for twenty-five years. Most recently she has acted as the Program Director for Kinder Konzerts with the FRIENDS of the Minnesota Orchestra. She has passed on her mothering advice as a mentor and speaker to mother's groups. She enjoys cooking for others in her home, and volunteering as a sous-chef for Loaves and Fishes, a non-profit that serves healthy meals to those in need. Ann lives and laughs with her husband, Steve, while waiting for grandchildren, in the Minneapolis-St. Paul area.

Help Make A Difference!

Thank you for purchasing my book!

I really appreciate all of your feedback,
And I love hearing what you have to say.

Please leave a helpful
REVIEW on Amazon.

Thank you so much!

—Ann Lahm

Made in the USA
Monee, IL
21 July 2020